START-UP
DESIGN AND TECHNOLOGY

EATING FRUIT AND VEGETABLES

Claire Llewellyn

Evans

Published by Evans Brothers Limited
2A Portman Mansions
Chiltern Street
London W1U 6NR

Reprinted 2007

© Evans Brothers Limited 2006

Produced for Evans Brothers Limited by
White-Thomson Publishing Ltd.,
Bridgewater Business Centre, 210 High Street,
Lewes, East Sussex BN7 2NH

Printed in China by WKT Co. Ltd.

Editor: Dereen Taylor
Consultants: Nina Siddall, Head of Primary School
Improvement, East Sussex; Norah Granger, former
primary head teacher and senior lecturer in Education,
University of Brighton
Designer: Leishman Design

British Library Cataloguing in Publication Data
Llewellyn, Claire
    Eating Fruit and Vegetables. - (Start-up design
    and technology)
    1. Nutrition - Juvenile literature
    I. Title
    613.2

ISBN: 978 0 237 53024 2

Acknowledgements:
Special thanks to the following for their help and
involvement in the preparation of this book: Staff and
pupils at Coldean Primary School, Brighton and Elm
Grove Primary School, Brighton.

Picture Acknowledgements:
Chris Fairclough 4 (bottom), 7 (bottom), 9 (bottom), 10,
11 (top), 12, 13, 14, 15 (top), 17, 20. Liz Price cover, title
page, 4 (top), 5, 6, 7 (top), 8, 9 (top), 11 (bottom), 15
(bottom), 18, 21.

Artwork:
Tom Price age 8, page 16; Hattie Spilsbury age 10,
page 19.

Contents

Examining fruit and vegetables

Dan and Emily are looking at fruit and vegetables. They examine the outside to find out if the skin is rough or smooth. Which ones smell?

◄ Which fruit and vegetables are juicy inside? Which ones have seeds? Which ones have a strong smell?

4

rough   smooth   smell

The children put their answers on a chart.

	kiwi fruit	avocado	melon	tomato
strong smell		✔	✔	
juicy inside	✔		✔	✔
seeds	✔	✔	✔	✔

Fruit and vegetables come in different colours. Look in the supermarket to see which colour is the most common.
How could you show this on a chart?

juicy   seeds   colours   5

Describing fruit and vegetables

There are many different words to describe fruit and vegetables.

"This tomato is small, red and round. It feels firm."

▲ Some words describe the way they look and feel.

"This mandarin smells tangy and has a sweet, fresh taste."

▲ Some words describe the way they smell and taste.

describe   feels   firm   look

"Cucumber feels wet. When you bite it, it's crunchy."

Some words describe the way they feel in your mouth.

crisp crunchy firm
small long stringy
juicy bumpy hard
sweet squashy
round sour

▶ **Which words would you choose to describe the fruit and vegetables in the picture?**

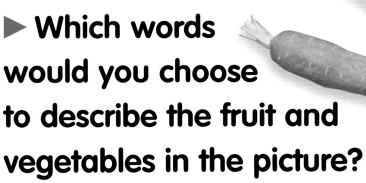

fresh   taste   bite   crunchy

Making fruit kebabs

Tom is making fruit kebabs out of kiwi fruits, apples and strawberries. Fruit kebabs are a healthy snack.

► Tom washes the fruit and drains it in a colander.

◄ Tom peels the kiwi fruit. He also chops the apples and slices the stalks off the strawberries.

HYGIENE!

Always wash your hands before touching food.

WARNING!

Knives and skewers are sharp. Use them with care.

.....8...... healthy   snack   washes   drains

► Tom mixes the fruit on wooden skewers. Which fruit kebab looks best? Why?

◄ Do you recognise the kitchen tools in the picture? What would you use them for?

Can you think up a new kitchen tool? What job would it do? How could you make it?

peels   chops   tools

Investigating packaging

Some fruit and vegetables are fresh. Others have been frozen, dried, tinned, or made into juice.

These foods are packaged to protect them from germs and bumps.
What kinds of packaging can you see in the picture?

frozen   dried   tinned

Kayla's class plan to sell fruit on Sport's Day. The fruit must look attractive and be clean and fresh. How could they package it?

► Which of these items of packaging could they use?

juice   packaging   attractive   11

Taste tests

We prepare fruit and vegetables in different ways. Some foods can be eaten raw. Ali is tasting some mashed, baked and fresh banana.

"This looks and tastes like baby food. I don't like it."

"This is warm and soft. It's ok, but the taste is a bit strong."

prepare   raw   mashed

"I enjoy eating bananas like this. They're yummy."

Why not try the following carrot taste test?

1 Raw carrot, washed and peeled.

2 Grated carrot, mixed with lemon juice and salt and pepper.

3 Boiled carrot.

Which do you think you would like best?

baked   grated   boiled

Making healthy soups and drinks

► Vegetables can be used to make soups. You can add pasta, too.

Some vegetable soups have bits in them. Other soups are put in a blender and whizzed until they are smooth. Which kind of soups do you prefer?

soups   blender   prefer

Fruit can be put in a blender, too. It can be mixed with milk or yogurt to make drinks called smoothies.

▼ Tom and Emily are having smoothies.

Which fruits would you like in your smoothie?

smoothies

A healthy diet

Fruit and vegetables are good for us. They help to keep us fit. They are part of a healthy diet.

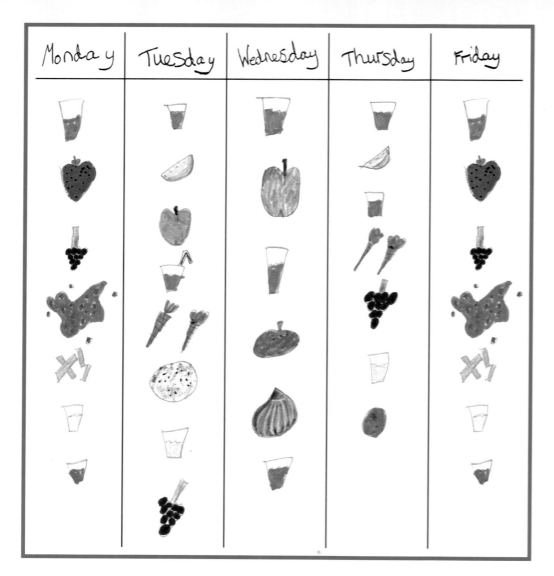

Monday	Tuesday	Wednesday	Thursday	Friday

◄ Fatima kept a fruit and vegetable diary. When did she eat the most fruit and vegetables? When did she eat the least?

Factbox

We should try to eat five pieces of fruit and vegetables a day.

fit   diet   most   least

► Fatima asked her friends how many fruit and vegetables they eat every day.

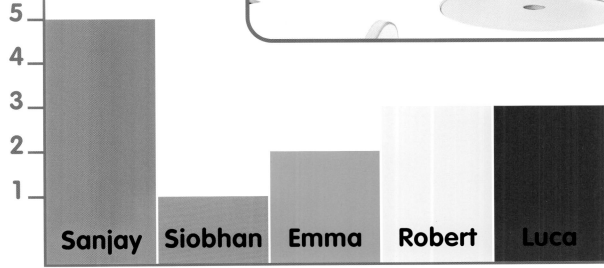

She made a bar chart of the results.
Who has five pieces a day? Who has just one?

pieces   bar chart

Planning a picnic

Ria's class are planning a Teddy Bears' Picnic.

"We need food like sandwiches that we can carry easily."

"I'd like some fruit juice in case I get thirsty."

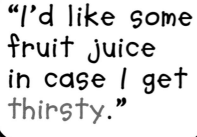

HYGIENE!

Wash your hands before touching food.

▶ They want to make sandwiches. They make lists of the things they will need.

Lettuce
Cheese
Butter
Bread

Colander
Chopping Board
Vegetable knife
Butter knife
Bread knife
Grater
plastic Box.

picnic   thirsty

How to make cheese and lettuce sandwiches

▲ **Wash and drain the lettuce.**

▲ **Butter the bread.**

▲ **Grate the cheese.**

▲ **Add some lettuce.**

▲ **Add another piece of bread and cut in half.**

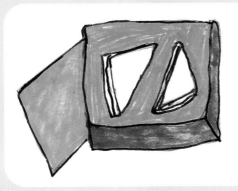

▲ **Put the sandwiches in a plastic box.**

WARNING! Knives are sharp. Use them with care.

carry   plastic

Choosing fruit for the picnic

Charmaine and Ali are thinking about fruit for the picnic. They want it to look and taste nice, and be easy to eat. They don't want fruit that will get squashed.

▲ Which of these fruits do you think would be best for the picnic?

easy   squashed

The children enjoy their Teddy Bears' Picnic.
What do they say about the food and drink?

water   **better**   **hungry**

Further information for

New words listed in the text:

attractive	crunchy	frozen	picnic	soups
baked	describe	grated	pieces	squashed
bar chart	diet	healthy	plastic	taste
better	drains	hungry	prefer	thirsty
bite	dried	juice	prepare	tinned
blender	easy	juicy	raw	tools
boiled	feels	least	rough	washes
carry	firm	look	seeds	water
chops	fit	mashed	smell	
colours	fresh	most	smooth	
		packaging	smoothies	
		peels	snack	

Possible Activities

PAGES 4-5

Collect pictures of fruit and vegetables and make a classroom display. Label each of the different foods.

Make a chart showing how many different green, red and yellow fruit and vegetables the children can think of. Which is the most common colour?

Ask the children to choose a fruit or vegetable and draw both the outside and the inside. Ask them to think up descriptive labels for the different parts - e.g. Kiwi fruit: 'Brown, furry skin'; 'Soft, green flesh'; 'Small black seeds'.

What is a vegetable? What is a fruit? Discuss the different definitions of each. Then, showing children a variety of fruit and vegetables, decide which are which. Children may be surprised to discover that tomatoes and peapods are both kinds of fruit.

PAGES 6-7

Collect pictures that could be the starting point for literacy work about fruit and vegetables. Make a list of words to suit each food. Can children guess the food from the words?

Read some poems about food. Ask the children to try writing their own poems about fruit and vegetables.

PAGES 8-9

Brainstorm all the different ways we eat fruit. Do children sometimes add sugar, custard and cream to fruit? How does this change the taste? Is it a healthy choice?

What other fruit combinations would be good for fruit kebabs? Ask the children to use drawings and labels to show how they would prepare the fruit and arrange it on the stick.

Ask children to design a poster telling people how to be clean and safe in the kitchen - e.g. 'Always wash your hands before touching food.'

PAGES 10-11

Visit a supermarket and investigate different forms of packaging e.g. for drinks. Which kind of packaging do the children think works best? Why?

Parents and Teachers

Visit the supermarket's greengrocery department, including the chiller cabinet. How does the supermarket make the fruit and vegetables look attractive? Does it use packaging? How?

PAGES 12-13

Organise taste tests. In one, children could compare shop-bought and home-produced food (e.g. shop-bought fresh fruit salad/canned fruit salad/home-made fruit salad). In another test, children could test a food that has been processed in different ways (e.g. raw, cooked and dried carrot or apple).

Potatoes can be prepared in many different ways. Ask the school cook how potatoes are served in school. Which is the healthiest? Which is the children's favourite?

PAGES 14-15

Brainstorm all the different soups that can be made with vegetables. Do a survey of the children's favourite soups and turn the results into a chart or pictogram.

Make a fruit smoothie (e.g. with strawberries, a banana, milk and yogurt). Then ask the children to write down the ingredients, and draw each step of the method.

PAGES 16-17

Have a fruit-tasting day. Ask all the children to bring in a piece of fruit, ensuring as wide a range as possible. Chop up the fruit to make a huge fruit salad that everyone can share.

OR

Prepare a mixed (vegetable) salad, using as many different foods as possible, and ask children to identify all the different ingredients.

Ask children to draw all the food they ate yesterday. How many pieces of fruit and vegetables did they eat?

Further Information

BOOKS FOR CHILDREN

Feeling Hungry? by Anita Ganeri (Evans, 2004)

Health and Growth (*Start-up Science*) by Claire Llewellyn (Evans, 2004)

Look After Yourself: Your Food by Claire Llewellyn (Franklin Watts, 2002)

Why Must I Eat Healthy Food? by Jackie Gaff (Evans, 2005)

Why Should I Eat Well? by Claire Llewellyn (Hodder Wayland, 2001)

WEBSITES

www.bbc.co.uk/health/kids

www.dole5aday.com/Kids/K_Index.jsp

www.5aday.com

PAGES 18-19 & 20-21

Plan your own Teddy Bears' Picnic. Ask the children to bring in a teddy bear and teach them the song 'If you go down to the woods today …' Ask them what they would like to eat and drink on a picnic (e.g. a sandwich and a drink). How would they go about making this? Ask them to list the foods and tools they will use and write or draw step-by-step instructions to plan their work.

Index